We Believe & Celebrate
First Communion

W9-CEK-095

Sadlier
A Division of William H. Sadlier, Inc.

Sadlier's *We Believe & Celebrate* program was developed by the community of faith through representatives with expertise in liturgy, theology, Scripture, catechesis, and children's faith development. This program leads to a deeper experience of Jesus in the community and springs from the wisdom of this community.

Catechetical and Liturgical Consultants

Dr. Gerard F. Baumbach
Director, Center for Catechetical Initiatives
Concurrent Professor of Theology
University of Notre Dame

Sr. Janet Baxendale, SC
Adjunct Professor of Liturgy
St. Joseph Seminary, Dunwoodie, NY

Carole M. Eipers, D.Min.
Executive Director of Catechetics
William H. Sadlier, Inc.

Rev. Ronald J. Lewinski, S.T.L.
St. Mary of the Annunciation
Mundelein, IL

Rev. Msgr. James P. Moroney
Executive Director of the USCCB
Secretariat for the Liturgy

Curriculum and Child Development Consultants

Patricia Andrews
Director of Religious Education
Our Lady of Lourdes
Slidell, LA

William Bischoff
Director of Catechetical Ministries
Mission San Luis Rey Parish
Oceanside, CA

Diana Carpenter
Director of Faith Formation
St. Elizabeth Ann Seton Parish
San Antonio, TX

Inculturation Consultants

Dulce M. Jimenez-Abreu
Director of Spanish Programs
William H. Sadlier, Inc.

Vilma Angulo
Director of Religious Education
All Saints Catholic Church
Sunrise, FL

Media/Technology Consultant

Sister Jane Keegan, RDC
Senior Internet Editor
William H. Sadlier, Inc.

Theological Consultants

Most Reverend Edward K. Braxton,
  Ph.D., S.T.D.
Official Theological Consultant
Bishop of Belleville

Monsignor John Arnold
Vicar General
Archdiocese of Westminster

Sadlier Consulting Team

Roy Arroyo
Michaela Burke
Judith Devine
Ken Doran
Kathleen Hendricks
William M. Ippolito
Saundra Kennedy, Ed.D.
Kathleen Krane
Suzan Larroquette

Writing/Development Team

Rosemary K. Calicchio
Vice President of Publications

Melissa Gibbons
Product Director

Blake Bergen
Editorial Director

MaryAnn Trevaskiss
Supervising Editor

Maureen Gallo
Senior Editor

Joanna Dailey
Editor

Publishing Operations Team

Deborah J. Jones
Vice President of Publishing Operations

Vince Gallo
Creative Director

Francesca O'Malley
Associate Art Director

Jim Saylor
Photography Manager

Design Staff
Andrea Brown
Sasha Khorovsky
Dmitry Kushnirsky

Production Staff
Barbara Brown
Vinny McDonough
Maureen Morgan
Gavin Smith
Kristine Walsh
Sommer Zakrzewski

Photo Credits

Cover Title Page: Neal Farris.
Interior: Jane Bernard 12, 14 *top*, 82 *top*, 82 *bottom*, 96. Karen Callaway 14 *bottom*, 82 *center*, 96 *top*. Crosiers/ Gene Plaisted, OSC 38 *top*. Neal Farris 13,15, 18, 25, 26, 27, 30, 36, 37, 42, 48, 49, 50, 51, 54, 60, 61, 62, 63, 66, 72, 74–75, 78, 84, 86 *top & bottom*, 88, 90, 92. Ken Karp 6, 65 *bottom left*. Punchstock/ Creatas 7. Veer 19, 31, 43, 55, 67. Bill Wittman 38 *bottom*, 39, 86 *center*.

Illustrator Credits

Tom Barrett: 72–73. Teresa Berassi: 60, 92. Mary Bono: 44, 45, 53, 68. Mircea Catusanu: 8, 9, 24, 42, 44, 49, 51. W.B. Johnston: 3, 6, 7, 12, 13–15, 19, 24, 26–28, 31, 37–39, 43, 54, 55, 62, 67, 74–77, 80, 82, 93–95. Dave Jonason: 45. Dean MacAdam: 18, 32, 33, 66, 86. Diana Magnuson: 10–11, 22–23, 34–35, 46–47, 58–59, 70–71, 81, 83, 85, 87, 89, 91, 95. Judith Moffatt: 16, 17, 41, 51. Gary Phillips: 4–5. Jackie Snider: 8, 20, 21, 30, 40, 41, 56, 57, 69, 94. Jessica Wolk-Stanley: 24, 86, 88, 90. Michael Woo: Mass punchouts.

Nihil Obstat

✠ Most Reverend Robert C. Morlino

Imprimatur

✠ Most Reverend Robert C. Morlino
Bishop of Madison
September 28, 2005

The Nihil Obstat and Imprimatur are official declarations that a book or pamphlet is free of doctrinal or moral error. No implication is contained therein that those who have granted the *Nihil Obstat* and *Imprimatur* agree with the contents, opinions, or statements expressed.

Acknowledgments

Excerpts from the English translation of *The Roman Missal,* © 2010, International Committee on English in the Liturgy, Inc. All rights reserved.

Scripture excerpts are taken from the *New American Bible with Revised New Testament and Psalms*. Copyright © 1991, 1986, 1970, Confraternity of Christian Doctrine, Inc. Washington, D.C. Used with permission. All rights reserved. No portion of the *New American Bible* may be reprinted without permission in writing from the copyright holder.

Excerpts from the English translation of *Rite of Baptism for Children* © 1969, ICEL. All rights reserved.

Excerpts from *Catholic Household Blessings and Prayers* Copyright © 1988, United States Catholic Conference, Inc. Washington, D.C. Used with permission. All rights reserved.

English translation of the *Kyrie, Gloria in Excelsis, Agnus Dei,* Nicene Creed, Apostles' Creed, and Lord's Prayer by the International Consultation on English Texts (ICET).

"We Believe, We Believe in God," © 1979, North American Liturgy Resources (NALR), 5536 NE Hassalo, Portland, OR 97213. All rights reserved. Used with permission. "We Celebrate with Joy," © 2000, Carey Landry. Published by OCP Publications, 5536 NE Hassalo, Portland, OR 97213. All rights reserved. Used with permission. "Take the Word of God with You," text © 1991, James Harrison. Music © 1991, Christopher Walker. Text and music published by OCP Publications, 5536 NE Hassalo, Portland, OR 97213. All rights reserved. Used with permission. "We Remember You," © 1999, Bernadette Farrell. Published by OCP Publications, 5536 NE Hassalo, Portland, OR 97213. All rights reserved. Used with permission. "Jesus, You Are Bread for Us," © 1988, Christopher Walker. Published by OCP Publications, 5536 NE Hassalo, Portland, OR 97213. All rights reserved. Used with permission.

William H. Sadlier, Inc.
9 Pine Street
New York, NY 10005-4700

ISBN: 978-0-8215-5718-1

8 9 10 11 RRDCH 18

CONTENTS

My Parish Church 4
Introduction 6

1 We Belong to the Church 7

Acts of the Apostles 2:1–4, 38–41 *Pentecost
and the Beginning of the Church*
Rite of Baptism; *Sacraments of Initiation*
Family Keepsake Pages 8–9, 16–17
Sharing Faith with My Family 81–82

2 We Gather and Give Thanks 19

Mark 11:8–9 *Jesus' Entry into Jerusalem*
Roman Missal; *Introductory Rites*
Family Keepsake Pages 20–21, 28–29
Sharing Faith with My Family 83–84

**3 We Celebrate the Liturgy of
the Word** 31

Matthew 13:3–8, 23 *The Parable of the Sower
and the Seed*
Roman Missal; *Liturgy of the Word*
Family Keepsake Pages 32–33, 40–41
Sharing Faith with My Family.................... 85–86

**4 We Celebrate the Liturgy of
the Eucharist** 43

Mark 14:22–24 *The Last Supper*
Luke 22:19
Roman Missal; *Liturgy of the Eucharist:
Preparation of the Gifts and Eucharistic Prayer*
Family Keepsake Pages 44–45, 52–53
Sharing Faith with My Family....................87–88

**5 We Receive the Body and
Blood of Christ** 55

Luke 24:13–35 *Jesus on the Road to Emmaus*
John 6:35; 14:27
Roman Missal; *Liturgy of the Eucharist:
Communion Rite*
Family Keepsake Pages 56–57, 64–65
Sharing Faith with My Family 89–90

6 We Love and Serve the Lord 67

Matthew 28:16–20 *The Commissioning of
the Disciples*
Roman Missal; *Concluding Rites*
Family Keepsake Pages 68–69, 76–77
Sharing Faith with My Family 91–92

Receiving Communion 79
Sharing Faith with My Family 1–6 81
Prayers 93
Punchouts: altar, heart, cross,
and lantern ....Back of Book

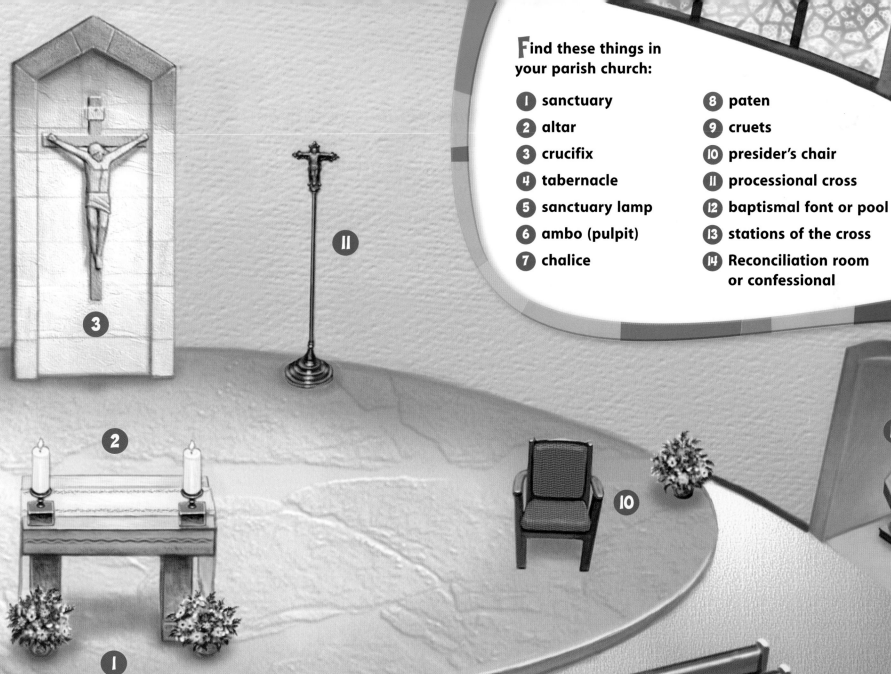

Find these things in your parish church:

1. sanctuary
2. altar
3. crucifix
4. tabernacle
5. sanctuary lamp
6. ambo (pulpit)
7. chalice
8. paten
9. cruets
10. presider's chair
11. processional cross
12. baptismal font or pool
13. stations of the cross
14. Reconciliation room or confessional

Welcome!

We Believe & Celebrate First Communion is your book. You will use it to prepare for your First Holy Communion. Many people will guide you as you learn about this special celebration in your life. So make this book one that you can keep forever.

As you go through each chapter you will:

✦ Gather and Share God's Word

You celebrate the people and things in your life. You read and listen to a story from the Bible.

✦ Believe and Celebrate

You learn about and prepare to receive the Sacrament of the Eucharist.

✦ Respond and Pray

With your family and friends you remember and celebrate what you believe. You celebrate your love for God in words and song.

Let's get started!

> "Receive the light of Christ."
>
> **Rite of Baptism**

We Gather

I belong to the _____ family.

My Family

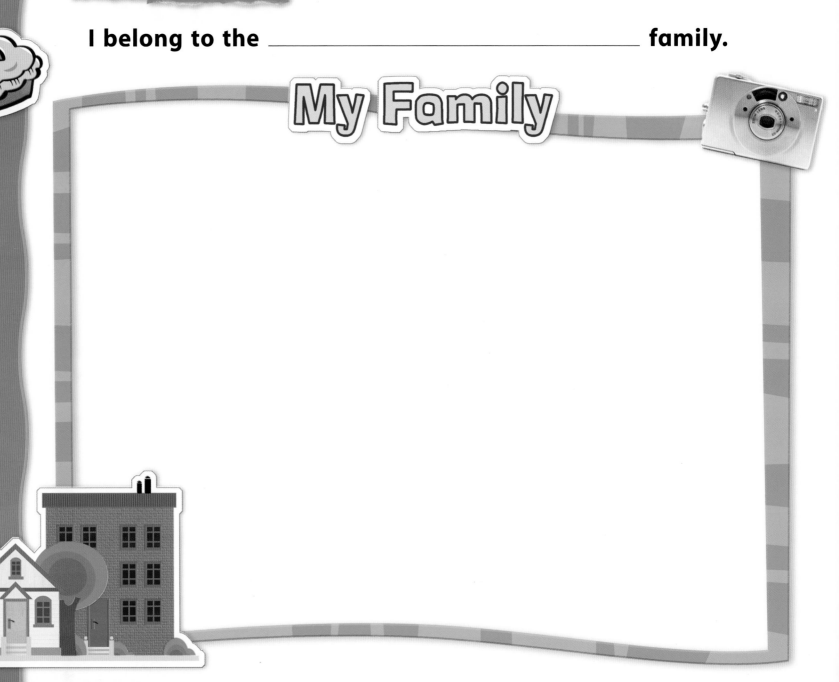

We show our love for one another by …

I love you

We Share God's Word

📖 Acts of the Apostles 2:1–4, 38–41

Narrator: Jesus told his disciples that he would return to his Father in heaven. But he said that the Holy Spirit would be with them to guide them. The Holy Spirit would help them remember everything that Jesus had said and done.

Jesus' Disciple: I was with the other disciples and with Mary, the mother of Jesus. Suddenly we heard a noise. It sounded like a strong wind. We saw what looked like a flame of fire over each one of us.

Narrator: "And they were all filled with the holy Spirit." (Acts of the Apostles 2:4)

Jesus' Disciple: We left where we were staying. Then Peter, one of Jesus' Apostles, began teaching. He invited the people to be baptized. He said that they, too, would then receive the Gift of the Holy Spirit.

Narrator: "Those who accepted his message were baptized, and about three thousand persons were added that day." (Acts of the Apostles 2:41)

We Believe and Celebrate

A community is a group of people who share with one another. They celebrate and work together.

The first community we belong to is our family. When we are baptized, we become a part of another community, the Church. The **Church** is all the people who are baptized in Jesus Christ and follow his teachings.

Through our Baptism, we belong to the Catholic Church. As Catholics, we believe in the Blessed Trinity. The Blessed Trinity is three Persons in one God, God the Father, God the Son, and God the Holy Spirit.

We believe that Jesus Christ, the Son of God, became one of us and died and rose again to save us. We try to love God and others as Jesus did. We do this through the help of the Holy Spirit.

There are members of the Catholic Church all over the world. Catholics gather together as parish communities to worship God and to share and celebrate God's love.

As Catholics we gather together in our parish community. We gather for Mass and the celebration of the sacraments. We gather to show our love for God and others.

THE SEVEN SACRAMENTS

Baptism

Confirmation

Eucharist

Penance and Reconciliation

Anointing of the Sick

Matrimony

Holy Orders

We Believe and Celebrate

A **sacrament** is a special sign given to us by Jesus. Every time we celebrate a sacrament, Jesus is with us through the power of the Holy Spirit. The prayers we pray and the things we do show that we are joined, or united, with Jesus. So through each sacrament we share in God's own life and love.

Through Baptism, God shares his life with us. We become children of God and members of the Church. We call God's life in us **grace**.

Baptism is the first sacrament we receive. At Baptism, we are placed in water or water is poured over our heads. The priest or deacon prays special words. We are baptized in the name of the Father, and of the Son, and of the Holy Spirit. When we are baptized, we are anointed with oil. This reminds us that we are receiving the Gift of the Holy Spirit for the first time.

In the Sacrament of Confirmation, we are sealed with the Gift of the Holy Spirit and strengthened. At Confirmation we are again anointed with oil. This shows that the Holy Spirit is with us in a very special way. It shows that we are set apart to do God's work.

In the Sacrament of the Eucharist, the bread and wine become the Body and Blood of Jesus Christ. We receive Jesus Christ himself in Holy Communion. We are united with Jesus Christ and to one another.

Baptism, Confirmation, and Eucharist are the sacraments of initiation. Another word for initiation is *beginning*. After we receive all three of these sacraments, we are full members of the Church.

We Respond

I am a member of the Catholic Church.

I was baptized in _____ Parish.

Today I belong to _____ Parish.

Together with my parish I . . .

This is my family celebrating my Baptism.

This is my family helping me prepare to receive Jesus in the Eucharist for the first time.

We Respond in Prayer

✝ **Leader:** Let us pray the Sign of the Cross together and join in singing.

🎵 **We Believe, We Believe in God**

Chorus
We believe in God;
we believe, we believe in Jesus;
We believe in the Spirit who gives us life.
We believe, we believe in God.

We believe in the Holy Spirit,
who renews the face of the earth.
We believe we are part of a living Church,
and forever we will live with God.

(Chorus)

Leader: Jesus, we are children of God and a part of your community, the Church. At Baptism we receive the light of Christ and promise to walk in your light.

All: Jesus, you are our light.

Leader: Jesus, thank you for your love. Also, thank you for the gift of the sacraments. We believe that it is through the seven sacraments that we share in God's own life.

All: Jesus, you are our light.

Leader: Let us join hands together as we pray the words Jesus taught us to pray.

All: Our Father…

We Gather and Give Thanks

"Glory to God in the highest."

Roman Missal

We Gather

My favorite family celebrations are ...

The celebration that is most special is . . .

It is most special because . . .

We Share God's Word

Jesus and his disciples often gathered to celebrate Jewish feasts and holy days. Together they thanked God the Father for his blessings.

For some feasts they went to the Temple in Jerusalem to celebrate with other Jewish families. The Temple was the holy place in Jerusalem where Jewish people prayed and worshiped God.

📖 Mark 11:8–9

The week before Jesus died and rose again, he and his disciples went up to Jerusalem. Many people were there to celebrate the important Jewish feast of Passover. People heard that Jesus and his disciples were coming to celebrate, too.

Many people went to meet Jesus. Some spread out their coats on the road. Others spread tree branches or waved them as Jesus passed. People began to praise Jesus. They called out,

"Hosanna!
    Blessed is he who comes in the name
      of the Lord!" (Mark 11:9)

23

We Believe and Celebrate

We gather with our parish community to celebrate God's love. We worship God together. To **worship** God means "to praise and thank" him.

Every Sunday we gather with our parish to worship God. We celebrate the Eucharist. This celebration of the Eucharist is called the **Mass**. By our special words and actions, we show that we believe that God is with us.

The community of people who join together for the celebration of the Mass is called the gathered **assembly**. A priest leads the gathered assembly in this celebration. He is called the celebrant. He is often assisted by a deacon. At Mass the priest and the deacon wear special clothing called vestments.

Our Sunday Celebration

It was on a Sunday that Jesus Christ rose to new life. So Sunday is a special day for the Church. We rest and worship God.

The Church tells us to worship God by taking part in the Mass every Sunday of the year. We are also to attend Mass on special days called holy days of obligation. When we do this we follow the third commandment and one of the laws of the Church.

Sunday is called the Lord's Day. The celebration of the Lord's Day is from Saturday evening through Sunday until midnight. During this time, as Catholics, we gather with our parish to celebrate the Mass. This celebration of the Eucharist is the center of Catholic life.

Throughout the Mass we show God our love by singing, praying, and listening to God's word. Together with the priest, we

✦ praise and thank God

✦ listen to God's word

✦ remember Jesus' life, death, Resurrection, and Ascension

✦ celebrate that Jesus gives himself to us in the Eucharist.

Our Parish Priests

Through the Sacrament of Holy Orders, a man becomes a priest. Many priests serve in local parishes. They spend their lives sharing God's love with people. They act in the Person of Christ in celebrating Mass and the other sacraments.

We Believe and Celebrate

The celebration of Mass begins with the **Introductory Rites**. These prayers and actions at the beginning of the Mass help us to remember that we are a worshiping community. They prepare us to listen to God's word and to celebrate the Eucharist.

Here is what we do during the Introductory Rites:

✦ We stand and sing to praise God. As we sing, the priest, deacon, and others helping at Mass walk to the altar. The priest and deacon kiss the altar as a sign of respect.

✦ We make the sign of the cross. Then the priest greets us. His words and our response remind us that Jesus is present with us.

- The priest asks us to think about times we have not loved God and others. Then we ask God and one another for forgiveness.

- Together with the priest we praise God for his love and forgiveness. We may pray:
    "Lord, have mercy."
    "Christ, have mercy."
    "Lord, have mercy."

- We often sing or say a prayer of praise to God the Father, God the Son, and God the Holy Spirit. This prayer begins with the words:
    "Glory to God in the highest,
        and on earth peace to people
        of good will."

- The priest prays an opening prayer. We respond, "Amen."

"Glory to God in the highest"

We Respond

When we gather with our parish for Mass, we often use these words to worship God ...

We use these prayerful actions ...

My family can pray to Jesus at home. We can make a special place of prayer where we can gather.

We Respond in Prayer

♫ We Celebrate with Joy

We celebrate with joy and gladness!
We celebrate God's love for us!
We celebrate with joy and gladness:
God with us today! God with us today!

✝ **Leader:** We place a bowl of holy water in the prayer space.

Reader 1: God, may this holy water remind us of our Baptism. At Baptism we became your children and members of the Church.

All: God our Father, we praise and thank you.

Leader: We place a cross here.

Reader 2: Jesus, may this cross remind us that you became one of us and died and rose again to save us from sin.

All: Jesus, Son of God, we praise and thank you.

Leader: We place a candle here.

Reader 3: Holy Spirit, may the candle flame remind us that you are with us to guide us.

All: God the Holy Spirit, we praise and thank you.

Leader: Let us join in praying words we often pray at Mass:

All: "Glory to God in the highest
and on earth peace to people
of good will.

We praise you, we bless you,
we adore you, we glorify you,
we give you thanks for your great
glory."

We Celebrate the Liturgy of the Word

"Praise to you, Lord
Jesus Christ."

Roman Missal

My favorite story is …

It is my favorite because …

y favorite Bible story is ...

It is my favorite because ...

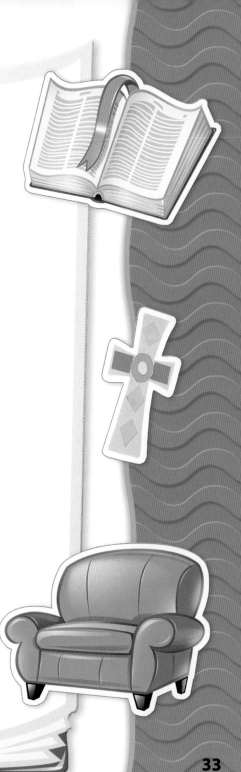

33

We Share God's Word

One day a large crowd gathered to hear Jesus teach. Jesus told them this story. You can read this story with your friends and family, too.

📖 Matthew 13:3–8, 23

Once there was a farmer who planted seeds. Some seeds did not fall in his field. They fell on a path. Birds came and ate these seeds.

Some seeds fell on rocky ground. The soil was not very deep. Plants began to grow. But then they dried up and died.

Other seeds fell into the thorns and weeds. Plants started to grow. But these plants were choked by the thorns and weeds.

"But some seed fell on rich soil." (Matthew 13:8) These seeds grew into strong, healthy plants, and produced fruit.

Jesus explained the meaning of his story. He said that people who listen carefully to God's word are like the seeds in the rich soil. They grow in God's love and share his love with others.

34

We Believe and Celebrate

The Bible is the book of God's word. The Bible has two parts, the Old Testament and the New Testament. In the Old Testament we learn about God's people who lived before Jesus' time on earth. In the New Testament we learn about Jesus and his disciples and about the beginning of the Church.

THE LITURGY OF THE WORD

First Reading

Responsorial Psalm

Second Reading

Alleluia (or other words of praise)

Gospel

Homily

Creed

Prayer of the Faithful

Every Sunday at Mass we listen to three readings from the Bible. We listen to God speaking to us through his word. This takes place during the Liturgy of the Word. The **Liturgy of the Word** is the part of the Mass in which we listen to God's word being proclaimed. *To proclaim* means "to announce God's word."

On most Sundays the first reading is from the Old Testament. From this reading we learn about the wonderful things God did for his people before Jesus was born. We learn that God's love for his people never ends.

Good News

A **psalm** is a song of praise from the Bible. After the first reading the reader or cantor prays a psalm verse. We sing or say a response.

The second reading is from the New Testament. During this reading we listen to the teachings of the Apostles. We learn about the beginning of the Church.

The third reading is the **Gospel**. It is from one of the four Gospels of the New Testament. The word *gospel* means "good news."

On most Sundays we sing Alleluia before the Gospel is read. When we listen to the Gospel, we learn the good news about Jesus Christ and his teachings.

We Believe and Celebrate

We praise and thank God during the Liturgy of the Word. We pray, "Thanks be to God," after the first and second readings. We pray, "Praise to you, Lord Jesus Christ," after the Gospel.

After we have heard all the readings, the priest or deacon talks to us about them. This talk is called the **homily**. When we listen carefully to the homily, we learn more about God. We learn ways we can share God's love with others.

When the homily is finished, we pray the **Creed**. We announce what we believe as Catholics. We believe in God the Father, God the Son, and God the Holy Spirit. We believe in the Church and in God's forgiveness of our sins.

After the Creed we pray the **Prayer of the Faithful**. We pray for the needs of all God's people.

Rejoice

We pray for the whole Church. We pray for the pope, other Church leaders, and all God's people. We pray for people throughout the world, especially for those who are sick or in need. We pray for the people in our parish who have died. We pray for people in our lives who need God's love and help. After each prayer, we ask God to hear our prayer.

When We Celebrate

At the Liturgy of the Word:

- A reader reads the first two readings. They are read from a book called the *Lectionary*. We sit while we listen to these readings.

- A priest or deacon reads from the Gospel of Matthew, Mark, Luke, or John. It is most often read from a special book called the *Book of the Gospels*. We stand as the Gospel is read as a sign of respect for God who is speaking to us.

We Respond

During the Liturgy of the Word, God's word is proclaimed.

I praise and thank God by ...

During the Prayer of the Faithful, we pray for all God's people.

This week I will pray for ...

My family and I listen to God's word at Mass. We can live out God's word this week by ...

We Respond in Prayer

✝ **Leader:** God, we thank you for the gift of your word.

All: O God, your word gives us life.

Leader: God, we believe you speak to us through your word.

All: O God, your word gives us life.

Leader: Let us stand and sing alleluia.

All: Alleluia!

Reader: A reading from the holy Gospel according to Matthew

(Read Matthew 13:3–8, 23)

The Gospel of the Lord.

All: Praise to you, Lord Jesus Christ.

Leader: Pray quietly. Talk to Jesus about listening to God's word. Ask the Holy Spirit to guide you in welcoming God's word into your heart.

🎵 **Take the Word of God with You**

Take the word of God with you
    as you go.
Take the seeds of God's word
    and make them grow.

Go in peace to serve the world,
    in peace to serve the world.
Take the love of God, the
    love of God with you as
    you go.

We Celebrate the Liturgy of the Eucharist

4

> "Let us give thanks
> to the Lord our God."
>
> **Roman Missal**

We Gather

I am thankful for ...

Things

People

44

Here are ways I can show that I am thankful ...

WOOF

We Share God's Word

📖 Mark 14:22–24

Narrator 1: Passover is an important feast that the Jewish people celebrate every year. During this holy time Jews gather together to remember all that God did for them. They share a special meal. At the meal they say prayers of blessing.

Narrator 2: On the night before Jesus died, he and his disciples were getting ready to celebrate the Passover.

Reader: Here is what Jesus said and did at the meal. "While they were eating, he took bread, said the blessing, broke it, and gave it to them, and said, 'Take it; this is my body.' Then he took a cup, gave thanks, and gave it to them, and they all drank from it. He said to them, 'This is my blood.'" (Mark 14:22–24)

Narrator 1: This was the last meal Jesus shared with his disciples before he died. We call this meal the Last Supper.

Narrator 2: At the Last Supper Jesus gave us the gift of the Eucharist. The Eucharist is the sacrament of the Body and Blood of Jesus Christ.

We Believe and Celebrate

Jesus told his disciples to remember what he had done at the Last Supper. He told them to remember and celebrate this special meal again and again. He said, "Do this in memory of me." (Luke 22:19) We do what Jesus asked each time we celebrate the Eucharist.

The Mass is the celebration of the Eucharist. The word *eucharist* means "to give thanks." Throughout the Mass, we give God thanks and praise.

The **Liturgy of the Eucharist** is the part of the Mass in which the bread and wine become the Body and Blood of Jesus Christ. The Liturgy of the Eucharist begins as the priest prepares the altar. Then members of the assembly bring forward the gifts of bread and wine. We remember the many gifts God has given to us. We get ready to offer these gifts and ourselves back to God. The word *offer* means "to give" or "to present."

THE LITURGY OF THE EUCHARIST

Preparation of the Gifts

Prayer over the Offerings

Eucharistic Prayer

Communion Rite

The priest or deacon accepts the gifts of bread and wine. He brings them to the altar. He prepares the gifts with special prayers. We respond, "Blessed be God for ever." Then we pray with the priest that the Lord will accept these gifts.

Throughout the Liturgy of the Eucharist, we remember that the Mass is a sacrifice. A **sacrifice** is an offering of a gift to God. As a sacrifice, Jesus offered his life for us on the cross to save us from sin. He rose to new life so that we could live happily with God forever. At every Mass, Jesus again offers himself to the Father.

The Eucharist is offered to make up for the sins of the living and the dead. Through it we receive spiritual and physical help from God.

We Believe and Celebrate

After the gifts are prepared, we pray the Eucharistic Prayer. The **Eucharistic Prayer** is the great prayer of praise and thanksgiving. This prayer is the most important prayer of the Church. It joins the members of the Church to Christ and to one another.

The priest prays the Eucharistic Prayer in the name of the whole Church. He prays to God the Father through Jesus Christ in the Holy Spirit.

Through the power of the Holy Spirit the priest says and does what Jesus said and did at the Last Supper.

Taking the bread the priest says:
"TAKE THIS, ALL OF YOU, AND EAT OF IT, FOR THIS IS MY BODY, WHICH WILL BE GIVEN UP FOR YOU."
Then taking the cup of wine he says:
"TAKE THIS, ALL OF YOU, AND DRINK FROM IT, FOR THIS IS THE CHALICE OF MY BLOOD...."

This part of the Eucharistic Prayer is called the **Consecration**.

"FOR THIS IS MY BODY"

"FOR THIS IS THE CHALICE OF MY BLOOD"

By the power of the Holy Spirit and through the words and actions of the priest, the bread and wine become the Body and Blood of Christ. Jesus Christ is really present in the Eucharist. We call this the *Real Presence*.

The priest invites us to proclaim our faith. We may pray: "When we eat this Bread and drink this Cup, we proclaim your Death, O Lord, until you come again."

We pray that the Holy Spirit will unite all who believe in Jesus. We end the Eucharistic Prayer by praying "Amen." When we do this, we are saying "Yes, I believe." We are saying "yes" to the prayer the priest has prayed in our name.

When We Celebrate

Only a priest ordained through the Sacrament of Holy Orders can preside at the Eucharist and consecrate the bread and wine. At Mass the priest uses a special plate and cup. The plate is called a *paten*. The priest places the wheat bread that becomes the Body of Christ on the paten. The cup is called a *chalice*. The priest pours the grape wine that becomes the Blood of Christ in the chalice.

51

We Respond

During this Sunday's Mass I will thank God especially for ...

During this week, my family will thank God especially for ...

We Respond in Prayer

✝ **Leader:** Let us lift our minds and hearts in prayer as we sing together.

🎵 **We Remember You**

Jesus, we remember you.
Jesus, we remember you.
We remember you gave your life for us.
We remember. We believe.

We praise you, we remember you.
We bless you, we remember you,
And we thank you that we belong to you.
We remember. We believe.

Leader: Jesus, thank you for the gift of yourself in the Eucharist.

All: Jesus, we thank you.

Leader: Jesus, thank you for your great sacrifice. Thank you for giving your life for us to save us from sin.

All: Jesus, we thank you.

Leader: As _____ prepares to
_(name or names)
receive Jesus in the Eucharist for the first time, we ask for your blessing.

"N., may the Lord Jesus touch your
  ears to receive his word,
and your mouth to proclaim his faith.
May you come with joy to his supper
to the praise and glory of God."

All: Amen. Jesus, we thank you.

5

We Receive the Body and Blood of Christ

"Blessed are those called to the supper of the Lamb."

Roman Missal

Sometimes people celebrate special events by sharing a meal.

One special event my family celebrated in this way was ...

The people who celebrated were ...

Here are some things we did at our celebration ...

We Share God's Word

Before he returned to his Father in heaven, the risen Jesus often visited his disciples.

📖 Luke 24:13–35

Reader 1: It was the Sunday that Jesus had risen from the dead. Two of Jesus' disciples were walking to Emmaus, a town near Jerusalem.

Reader 2: A man met the disciples on the road. He started walking with them. They did not know that this man was the risen Jesus.

Reader 3: The disciples told him that they were talking about the past three days. Jesus was crucified, died, and was buried. And now his body was missing from the tomb.

Reader 4: It was getting dark when they reached the town. The disciples asked the man to stay with them. He did stay. "While he was with them at table, he took bread, said the blessing, broke it, and gave it to them." (Luke 24:30)

Reader 5: Then the disciples recognized that this man was the risen Jesus! They knew him "in the breaking of the bread." (Luke 24:35)

In the Liturgy of the Eucharist, after the Eucharistic Prayer, we prepare to receive Jesus himself in Holy Communion. Our gifts of bread and wine have now become the Body and Blood of Christ. And we will receive the Body and Blood of Christ in Holy Communion.

We join ourselves with the whole Church as we pray aloud or sing the Lord's Prayer.

Then the priest reminds us of Jesus' words at the Last Supper. Jesus said, "Peace I leave with you; my peace I give to you." (John 14:27)

We pray that Christ's peace may be with us always. We share a sign of peace with the people who are near us. When we do this we show that we are united to Jesus Christ and to one another.

After we share a sign of peace, we pray to Jesus who sacrificed his life to save us from sin. We ask him for forgiveness and peace. We begin the prayer with these words:

"Lamb of God, you take away
the sins of the world,
have mercy on us."

As we pray the Lamb of God, the priest breaks the Bread, the Host, that has become the Body of Christ.

We Believe and Celebrate

After we pray the Lamb of God, the priest invites us to receive Jesus Christ in Holy Communion. The priest says,
"Behold the Lamb of God,
behold him who takes away the sins of the world.
Blessed are those called to the supper of the Lamb."

Together with the priest we pray,
"Lord, I am not worthy that you should enter under my roof,
but only say the word and my soul shall be healed."

Then we go forward with love and respect to receive Jesus in Holy Communion. As each person approaches, the priest, deacon, or extraordinary minister of Holy Communion raises the Host. The person bows his or her head. The priest, deacon, or extraordinary minister says, "The Body of Christ." The person responds "Amen" and then receives the Host.

If the person is receiving from the chalice, the priest, deacon, or extraordinary minister of Holy Communion raises the chalice. The person bows his or her head. The priest, deacon, or extraordinary minister says, "The Blood of Christ." The person responds, "Amen" and drinks from the cup.

As the gathered assembly receives the Body and Blood of Christ, we sing a song of thanksgiving. We are united with the whole Church.

Then there is usually some quiet time. During this time we remember that Jesus is present within us. We thank Jesus for the gift of himself in Holy Communion.

We Respond

The people in my parish who are helping me to prepare for my First Holy Communion are ...

I can thank them by ...

My friends and family who will be with me as I receive First Holy Communion are ...

On the day of my First Holy Communion I will ...

We Respond in Prayer

✝ **Leader:** Let us pray together the Lord's Prayer. As we pray, let us remember that through the Eucharist we are joined to Jesus and the whole Church.

All: Our Father . . . .

Leader: Let us pray for the people of our parish who are helping us prepare for First Holy Communion.

All: Jesus, thank you for our parish community's help during this special time.

Leader: Jesus said, "I am the bread of life." (John 6:35) We need bread to live and grow. We need Jesus to grow closer to God and to share in God's life. In Holy Communion, we receive Jesus, the Bread of Life.
Let us bow our heads and thank Jesus for the gift of himself in Holy Communion.

All: Jesus, thank you for the gift of yourself in Holy Communion.

Leader: Let us sing together.

🎵 **Jesus, You Are Bread for Us**

Jesus, you are bread for us.
Jesus, you are life for us.
In your gift of Eucharist we find love.
When we feel we need a friend,
    you are there with us, Jesus.
Thank you for the friend you are.
Thank you for the love we share.

"May almighty God bless you."

Roman Missal

Here are ways the people in my family show their love and care for others...

Here are ways my friends and neighbors show their love and care for others ...

We Share God's Word

📖 Matthew 28:16–20

Reader 1: After Jesus had risen from the dead, eleven of his disciples gathered on a mountain in Galilee. Jesus had sent them a message to meet him there.

Reader 2: When the disciples saw Jesus, they could hardly believe their eyes. Then Jesus said, "All power in heaven and on earth has been given to me. Go, therefore, and make disciples of all nations, baptizing them in the name of the Father, and of the Son, and of the holy Spirit." (Matthew 28:18–19)

Reader 1: Jesus wanted his disciples to share God's love with all people. Jesus wanted his disciples to teach others how to be his followers and friends.

Reader 2: Then Jesus promised his disciples that he would always be present with them. He said, "I am with you always." (Matthew 28:20)

We Believe and Celebrate

Go in Peace

Jesus sent his disciples out to continue his work. We are disciples of Jesus. He wants us to keep doing his work, too. He wants us to share God's love with others in our homes, schools, parishes, neighborhoods, cities or towns, and throughout the world. God's grace helps us to do all that he asks.

The celebration of the Mass ends with the **Concluding Rites**. At the end of Mass, together with the priest, we ask the Lord to be with us. Then the priest gives us a blessing. He says,

"May almighty God bless you, the Father, and the Son, † and the Holy Spirit."

We respond, "Amen."

Then the priest or deacon sends us out to share God's love with others. He may say, "Go in peace."

We respond, "Thanks be to God."

We sing a song as everyone leaves the church. All through the week we remember Jesus' promise to be with us always.

The word *Mass* comes from a word that means "to send out." The priest or deacon sends us out to continue Jesus' work by saying one of the following:

- "Go in peace."
- "Go forth, the Mass is ended."
- "Go and announce the Gospel of the Lord."

Saint Benedict Catholic Church

We Believe and Celebrate

Every Sunday we are joined to Jesus and the whole Church in the Sacrament of the Eucharist. We receive Jesus in Holy Communion, and our friendship with him grows. Our venial sins are forgiven and we are helped to stay away from serious sin.

Through the Holy Spirit, Jesus is with us as we continue his work all through the week. Receiving Jesus in Holy Communion helps us to love God and others. We become stronger disciples of Jesus. This helps us to join our parish community in loving and serving God and others.

We can love and serve God and others in many ways. Here are a few of those ways:

✦ help out at home or in school

✦ do something kind for a friend or neighbor

✦ give to a food or clothing drive

✦ send a get-well card or make a visit to someone who is sick

✦ pray for others, and especially people who are poor or hungry

✦ forgive others or ask for their forgiveness.

Most Blessed Sacrament

At Mass, after Holy Communion, there may be consecrated Hosts that have not been received. These Hosts are placed in the tabernacle and are called the Most Blessed Sacrament. The Most Blessed Sacrament is another name for the Eucharist.

We can visit the church and pray to Jesus who is present in the Most Blessed Sacrament. We can ask Jesus to help us love and care for others.

We Respond

With our parish community, our family can join in helping others.

Here are things we can do this week ...

PRAY FOR PEACE

Here is my family's prayer for peace …

Here are some ways my family will share Christ's peace this week …

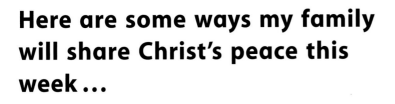

We Respond in Prayer

✝ **Leader:** Jesus, this is a very special time for us. This is because we are getting ready to receive our First Holy Communion. Help us to share God's gifts of love and peace with others during this special time.

All: Jesus, we are your friends and followers. Help us to remember that you are with us now and always.

Leader: Let us bow our heads and ask for God's blessing.

May God the Father,
Jesus Christ, the Son of God,
and God the Holy Spirit bless us.

All: Amen.

Leader: Let us go now in
peace to love one another.

All: Thanks be to God.

♫ Take the Word of God with You

Take the peace of God with you
as you go.

Take the seeds of God's peace
and make them grow.

Chorus
Go in peace to serve the world,
in peace to serve the world.
Take the love of God, the love of God
with you as you go.

Other Verses
✦ Take the joy of God with you as you go.

✦ Take the love of God with you as you go.

How to Receive Jesus in Holy Communion

When I receive the consecrated bread, or Host, this is what I do:

I walk to the altar with hands joined.

I think about Jesus, whom I will receive.

As my turn comes, the priest, deacon, or extraordinary minister of Holy Communion raises the Host, and I bow my head.

When I hear the words, "The Body of Christ," I respond, "Amen." I can choose to receive the Host in my hand or on my tongue.

If I choose to receive the Host in my hand, I cup my left hand on top of my right hand (or the opposite if I am left-handed). After the Host is placed in my hand, I step to the side and carefully place it in my mouth. I swallow the Host and return to my seat.

If I choose to receive the Host on my tongue, I hold my head up and gently put out my tongue. After the Host is placed on my tongue, I step to the side, swallow it, and return to my seat.

I bow my head.

I receive the Host in my hand.

or

I receive the Host on my tongue.

If I am going to receive from the chalice, I first swallow the Host. I move to the priest or extraordinary minister of Holy Communion holding the chalice.

The priest, deacon, or extraordinary minister raises the chalice, and I bow my head.

When I hear the words, "The Blood of Christ," I respond, "Amen."

Then I take a sip from the chalice.

After I receive Communion, this is what I do:

Sing the Communion chant, or song, with my parish family.

Spend time in quiet prayer.

I receive from the chalice.

Eucharistic Fast

As a sign of respect and reverence for Jesus in the Eucharist, we must have not taken any food or drink for one hour before receiving Holy Communion. This is called the eucharistic fast. Water and medicine may be taken during the eucharistic fast.

Leading a Sacramental Life

Receive Holy Communion often and the Sacrament of Penance regularly. Follow the laws of the Church which say: We must receive Holy Communion at least once a year during the Lenten/Easter season. We must confess our sins once a year if we have committed mortal, or serious, sin.

When we receive Holy Communion, we must always be in the state of grace. Anyone who has committed a mortal sin must receive absolution in the Sacrament of Penance before receiving Holy Communion.

"And they were all filled with the holy Spirit."

(Acts of the Apostles 2:4)

Talk about ways the first Church members shared God's love.

1 Sharing What I Learned

Look at the pictures and statements below. Match them. Use each match to tell your family what you learned in this chapter.

● As Catholics we gather together in our parish community for Mass and the celebration of the sacraments.

● Through Baptism we become children of God and members of the Church.

● At Confirmation we are sealed with the Gift of the Holy Spirit and strengthened.

Unscramble the words. Use the words to complete the sentences.

hrCuhc	camtnsrae	acrge

We call God's life in us

_____.

The _____ is all the people who are baptized in Jesus Christ and follow his teaching.

A _____ is a special sign given to us by Jesus.

"Blessed is he who comes in the name of the Lord!"

(Mark 11:9)

Talk about what people did to welcome Jesus to Jerusalem.

2 Sharing What I Learned

Look at the pictures and statements below. Match them. Use each match to tell your family what you learned in this chapter.

● During the Introductory Rites, the priest, deacon, and others helping at Mass walk to the altar.

● A priest leads the gathered assembly in the celebration of the Mass.

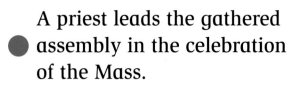

● Every Sunday we gather with our parish community to worship God.

Circle every other letter. Find the word that completes the sentence.

When we _____ God we "praise and thank" him.

In the window draw your family praising and thanking God.

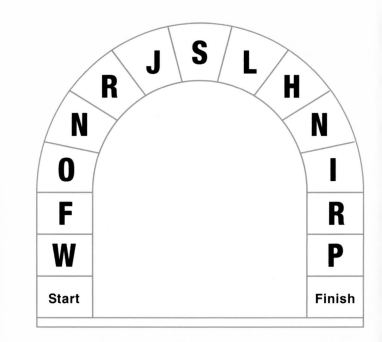

"But some seed fell on rich soil."

(Matthew 13:8)

Jesus explained the meaning of the story about a farmer who planted seeds. Talk about what Jesus said.

3 Sharing What I Learned

Look at the pictures and statements below. Match them. Use each match to tell your family what you learned in this chapter.

We listen to learn about the things God did for his people before Jesus was born.

We listen to the Gospel to learn the good news about Jesus.

After the homily we pray the Creed, announcing what we believe as Catholics.

Use the code to find the answer.

The word *gospel* means

86

"Do this in memory of me."

(Luke 22:19)

Talk about what Jesus did
at the Last Supper.

Sharing What I Learned

Look at the pictures and statements below. Match them. Use each match to tell your family what you learned in this chapter.

During the Liturgy of the Eucharist the members of the assembly bring forward the gifts of bread and wine.

At the Consecration, by the power of the Holy Spirit and through the words and actions of the priest, the bread and wine become the Body and Blood of Jesus Christ.

At the end of the Eucharistic Prayer, the priest prays in the name of the whole Church. We respond by praying, "Amen."

Find the words that complete this sentence. Use one color to fill in the "X" spaces.

During the Liturgy of the Eucharist, the bread and wine become the Body

and Blood of _____.

They knew him "in the breaking of the bread."

(Luke 24:35)

Talk about what happened when Jesus' disciples reached Emmaus.

Look at the pictures and statements below. Match them. Use each match to tell your family what you learned in this chapter.

After the Eucharistic Prayer, we pray the Lord's Prayer and share a sign of peace.

As the priest breaks the Bread, the Host, we pray the Lamb of God. We are praying to Jesus who sacrificed his life to save us from sin.

When we receive Holy Communion, we receive the Body and Blood of Christ.

Write a prayer to say after receiving Jesus in Holy Communion. Then decorate the frame and add a photo.

"Go, therefore, and make disciples of all nations."

(Matthew 28:18)

Talk about what Jesus wanted his disciples to do after he returned to his Father in heaven.

91

Look at the pictures and statements below. Match them. Use each match to tell your family what you learned in this chapter.

● During the Concluding Rites the priest gives us a blessing.

● The priest or deacon sends us out to share God's love with others. We sing a song as we leave the church.

● When we receive Holy Communion we become stronger disciples of Jesus.

Use the letters in the word "peace" to tell how you can share God's love and peace with others. One is done for you.

P
_____

forgivE
_____

A
_____

C
_____

E
_____

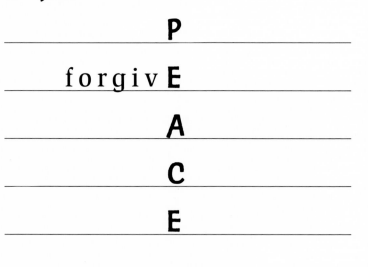

Nicene Creed

I believe in one God,
the Father almighty,
maker of heaven and earth,
of all things visible and invisible.

I believe in one Lord Jesus Christ,
the Only Begotten Son of God,
born of the Father before all ages.
God from God, Light from Light,
true God from true God,
begotten, not made, consubstantial
with the Father;
through him all things were made.
For us men and for our salvation
he came down from heaven,
and by the Holy Spirit was incarnate
of the Virgin Mary,
and became man.

For our sake he was crucified
under Pontius Pilate,
he suffered death and was buried,
and rose again on the third day
in accordance with the Scriptures.
He ascended into heaven
and is seated at the right hand
of the Father.
He will come again in glory to judge
the living and the dead
and his kingdom will have no end.

I believe in the Holy Spirit, the Lord,
the giver of life,
who proceeds from the Father and the Son,
who with the Father and the Son is
adored and glorified,
who has spoken through the prophets.
I believe in one, holy, catholic
and apostolic Church.
I confess one Baptism for the
forgiveness of sins
and I look forward to the resurrection
of the dead
and the life of the world to come.
Amen.

Apostles' Creed

I believe in God, the Father almighty,
Creator of heaven and earth,
and in Jesus Christ, his only Son, our Lord,
who was conceived by the Holy Spirit,
born of the Virgin Mary,
suffered under Pontius Pilate,
was crucified, died and was buried;
he descended into hell;
on the third day he rose again from
      the dead;
he ascended into heaven,
and is seated at the right hand
    of God the Father almighty;
from there he will come to judge
      the living and the dead.

I believe in the Holy Spirit,
    the holy catholic Church,
    the communion of saints,
    the forgiveness of sins,
    the resurrection of the body,
    and life everlasting.
Amen.

Our Father

Our Father, who art in heaven,
hallowed be thy name;
thy kingdom come;
thy will be done on earth
    as it is in heaven.
Give us this day our daily bread;
and forgive us our trespasses
as we forgive those
    who trespass against us;
and lead us not into temptation,
but deliver us from evil.
Amen.

Prayer Before Communion

Jesus, you are the Bread of Life.
Thank you for sharing your life with me.
Help me always to be your friend
and disciple.

Jesus, help me to welcome you into
my heart.
Help me to be true to you always.

Prayer After Communion

Jesus, you do such great things for me!
You fill me with your life.
Help me to grow in loving you and others.

Jesus, thank you for coming to me in
Holy Communion.
I love you very much. You come to live
within me.
You fill me with your life.
Help me to be and do all that you wish.

Prayer Before the Most Blessed Sacrament

Jesus,
you are God-with-us,
especially in this Sacrament of the Eucharist.
You love me as I am and help me grow.

Come and be with me
in all my joys and sorrows.
Help me share your peace and love
with everyone I meet.
I ask in your name.
Amen.

Dashed lines indicate folds

1. Carefully press out wall panel along perforations. Fold along dashed lines and push cross and candle panels halfway out as shown in picture ①.

2. Press out altar panel along perforations. Fold along dashed lines as shown in picture ②. Be sure to fold back **tabs C** and **D** and insert into **slots C** and **D** on floor of altar panel indicated by red arrows in picture ②. Push out and fold up chalice at base.

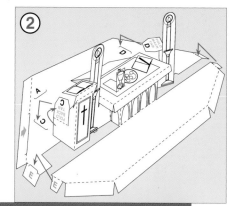

A

B

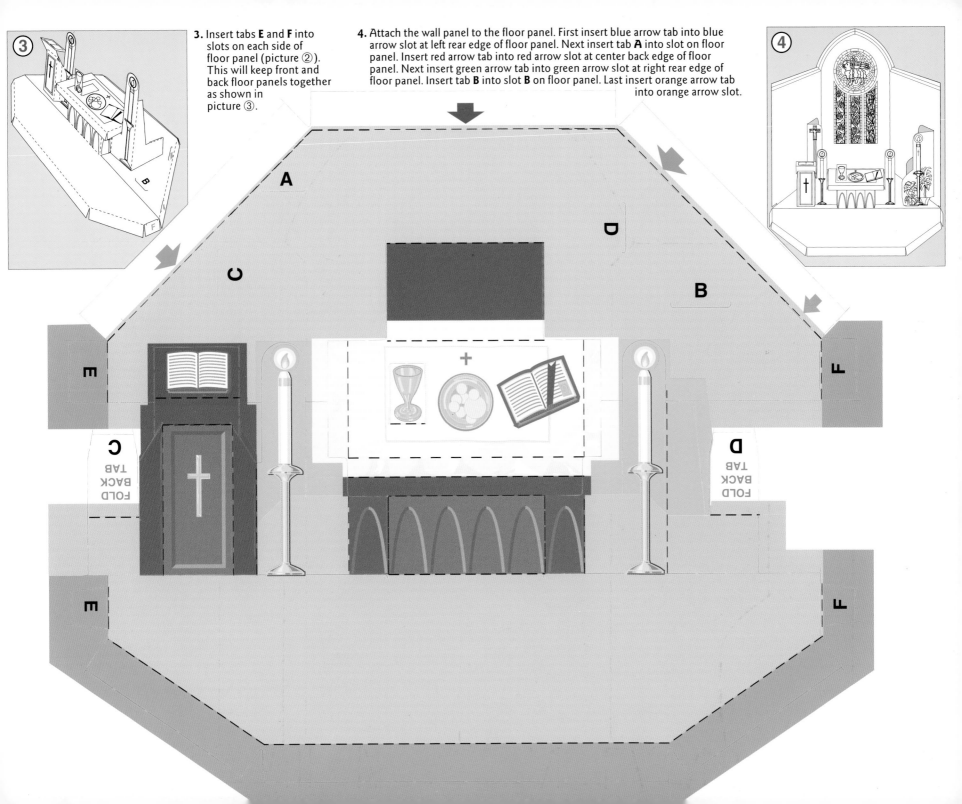

3. Insert tabs **E** and **F** into slots on each side of floor panel (picture ②). This will keep front and back floor panels together as shown in picture ③.

4. Attach the wall panel to the floor panel. First insert blue arrow tab into blue arrow slot at left rear edge of floor panel. Next insert tab **A** into slot on floor panel. Insert red arrow tab into red arrow slot at center back edge of floor panel. Next insert green arrow tab into green arrow slot at right rear edge of floor panel. Insert tab **B** into slot **B** on floor panel. Last insert orange arrow tab into orange arrow slot.

③

④

A

D

C

B

E

F

C
FOLD
BACK
TAB

D
FOLD
BACK
TAB

E

F

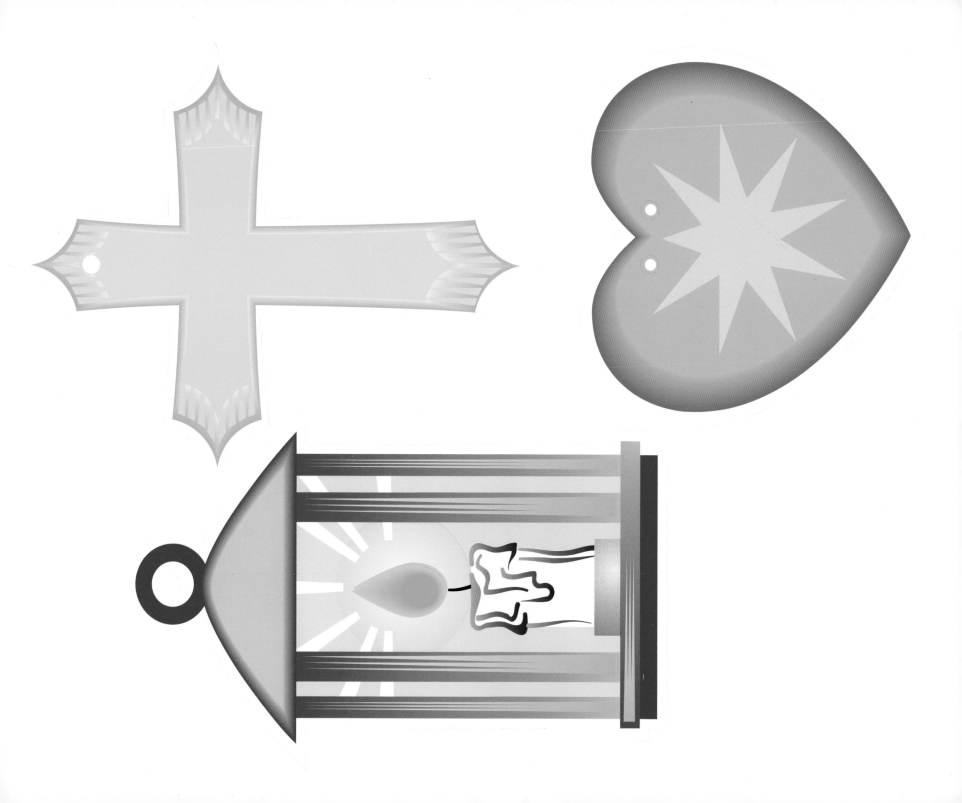

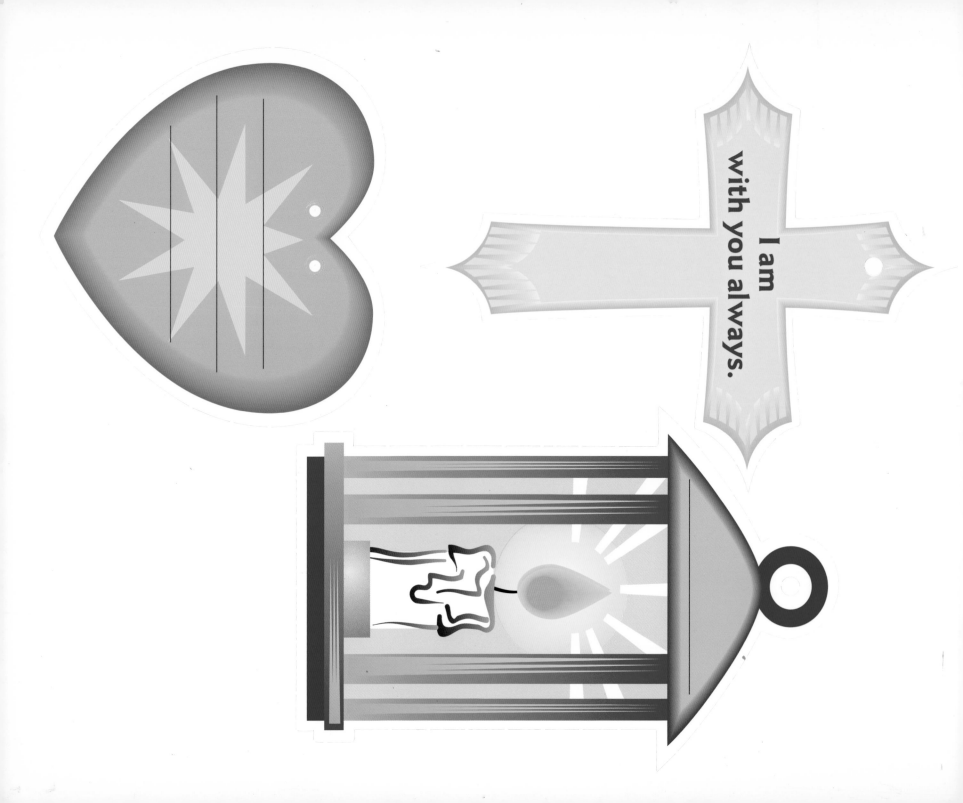

I am
with you always.